The Anne of Green Gables DIARY

This diary belongs to:

Name

Address

Telephone

"After all," Anne had said to Marilla once,
"I believe the nicest and sweetest days are not
those on which anything very splendid or
wonderful or exciting happens but just those
that bring simple little pleasures, following one
another softly, like pearls slipping off a string."
Life at Green Gables was full of just such days,
for Anne's adventures and misadventures, like
those of other people, did not all happen at once,
but were sprinkled over the year, with long
stretches of harmless, happy days between, filled
with work and dreams and laughter and lessons.

Anne of Avonlea

The Anne of Green Gables DIARY

*Featuring selections
from the Anne books
by L.M. Montgomery.*

*Compiled by Shelley Tanaka
Illustrated by Wes Lowe*

A Madison Press Book
produced for
Bantam-Seal

Published in Canada by Seal Books, 105 Bond St., Toronto, Ontario M5B 1Y3

Published in the United States of America by Bantam Books Inc., 666 Fifth Avenue, New York, N.Y., 10103.

Design: Falcom Design and Communications

**Produced by
Madison Press Books
40 Madison Avenue
Toronto, Ontario
Canada M5R 2S1**

Printed in Canada.

Introduction

Ever since *Anne of Green Gables* was first published in 1908, millions of readers all over the world have read and loved the Anne books. Though the stories are about a young girl who lived almost one hundred years ago, *Anne of Green Gables* remains one of the most popular and famous children's books in the world. In Japan, for instance, one million copies of *Anne of Green Gables* have been sold, and there are two L. M. Montgomery fan clubs. Anne Shirley is smart, funny, full of dreams and ambitions, and adults and young readers everywhere can identify with her triumphs and disappointments. We want to read the books over and over again.

Anne always wanted to be a writer. As a young girl, she formed a story club with her friends. She loved to read and she was always making up tales and giving names to her favorite trees and haunts. Anne's creator, L. M. Montgomery, kept a diary from the time she was a young girl — notebooks and journals in which she wrote poetry and short stories as well as descriptions of her cats, favorite places, visits with friends and relatives, school, and even reviews of books she had read.

Like L. M. Montgomery, you can use this diary as a notebook for your own poems and short stories, as a journal to write about school, your friends and your family, or as a place to keep your feelings and thoughts, make lists, or just doodle and scribble while you daydream. It is an undated diary so you can start on any day and use it all year. At the beginning of each month there is a *Things to Do* page where you can write down appointments, birthdays, holidays and special events. And throughout the diary there are quotes, illustrations and features to remind you of the Anne books, and tell you more about Anne and L. M. Montgomery.

For Anne, one of the best things about life was that she never knew what each new day would bring. "There is no such thing as a common day," she once said. "Every day has something about it no other day has." This diary will give you a place to keep a record of *your* days. I hope you will use it often and that it will make you want to read the Anne books, and reread them, just as I have done many times.

Shelley Tanaka
Toronto, Canada

Shelley Tanaka is an editor and author of children's books. She has loved the Anne books ever since she first read them when she was eleven years old.

Wes Lowe, the Canadian artist who drew the pictures for this diary, took great care to make them true to L.M. Montgomery's descriptions.

"January so far has been a month of cold gray days, with an occasional storm whirling across the harbor and filling Spook's Lane with drifts. But last night we had a silver thaw and today the sun shone. My maple grove was a place of unimaginable splendors. Even the commonplaces had been made lovely. Every bit of wire fencing was a wonder of crystal lace."

Anne of Windy Poplars

Things to do in
*J*ANUARY *19*___

Date		16	
1		17	
2		18	
3		19	
4		20	
5		21	
6		22	
7		23	
8		24	
9		25	
10		26	
11		27	
12		28	
13		29	
14		30	
15		31	

"When you hear a name pronounced can't you always see it in your mind, just as if it was printed out? I can; and A-n-n looks dreadful, but A-n-n-e looks so much more distinguished. If you'll only call me Anne spelled with an *e* I shall try to reconcile myself to not being called Cordelia."

Anne of Green Gables

...they all crowded into the big pung sleigh, among straw and furry robes. Anne reveled in the drive to the hall, slipping along over the satin-smooth roads with the snow crisping under the runners. There was a magnificent sunset, and the snowy hills and deep blue water of the St. Lawrence Gulf seemed to rim in the splendor like a huge bowl of pearl and sapphire brimmed with wine and fire. Tinkles of sleigh bells and distant laughter, that seemed like the mirth of wood elves, came from every quarter.

"Oh, Diana," breathed Anne, squeezing Diana's mittened hand under the fur robe, "isn't it all like a beautiful dream?..."

Anne of Green Gables

_____

_____

_____

_____

_____

_____

_____

_____

_____

_____

_____

_____

_____

_____

_____

_____

_____

_____

_____

_____

_____

_____

_____

_____

"I have a little brown cocoon of an idea that
may possibly expand into a magnificent moth of
fulfilment."

Anne's House of Dreams

"Oh, I know I'm a great trial to you, Marilla," said Anne repentantly. "I make so many mistakes. But then just think of all the mistakes I don't make, although I might."

Anne of Green Gables

Prince Edward Island

L. M. Montgomery once said that if it had not been for her own childhood in Prince Edward Island, she could never have written the Anne books. She spent much of her adult life in Ontario, but almost all of her books are set in Prince Edward Island. Anne's closeness to nature and the outdoors, her love of the sea, and her strong sense of family and community all come from living on the Island. Although there is no such place as Avonlea, it is very similar to Cavendish, the farming settlement on the north shore where L. M. Montgomery was raised.

Prince Edward Island, Canada's smallest province, is a crescent-shaped island just 140 miles long, located in the Gulf of St. Lawrence (its early Indian name, Abegweit, means "land cradled on the waves"). Because the Island is so narrow, no spot is far from the sea—at high tide, even the rivers are salt water for many miles inland.

Since P.E.I. is small and isolated, Islanders have a strong sense of homeland. Families have lived there for several generations, and many are of British, Irish and Scottish descent (L. M. Montgomery's own family came from Scotland). Although Prince Edward Island has changed since Anne's day, there are still a lot of villages like Avonlea, where families are close-knit, the church is an important part of life, and the sense of community is strong. Up until just a few decades ago, every small community still had its own one- or two-room schoolhouse like the one Anne attended and later taught at—now children are bused to larger regional schools.

Farming and fishing are the main industries of P.E.I. Although Avonlea was a farming settlement, Anne later lived in "Four Winds," a small fishing village typical of many seaside communities, guarded by its white wooden lighthouse built on a cliff that jutted out into the gulf, overlooking the harbor and sandbar on one side and the windswept sand dunes on the other. There are still more than sixty lighthouses around the Island, though only three are still manned.

In the Island's capital, Charlottetown, is the Confederation Centre of the Arts, where the musical "Anne of Green Gables" has been performed at the summer festival every year since 1965. The musical has also toured across Canada and in London, England, New York and Japan.

Everyone who has been to Prince Edward Island remarks how beautiful, peaceful and easy-going it is. The dirt roads are still a rich, reddish brown, due to the iron-oxide in the soil that rusts when it is exposed to the air. There are miles of rolling hillside and white sandy beaches. When the flower-loving British immigrants arrived in the 1800's, they planted roses, lupins and peonies, which now grow wild in many places on the Island. Prince Edward Island is still, as Anne once described it, "the bloomiest place."

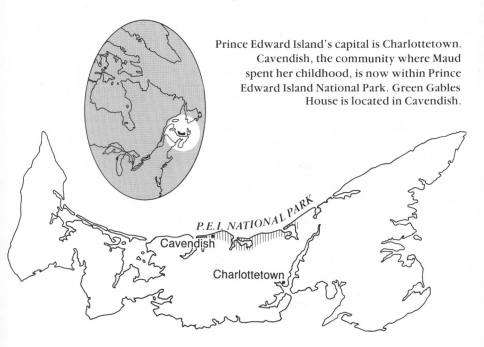

Prince Edward Island's capital is Charlottetown. Cavendish, the community where Maud spent her childhood, is now within Prince Edward Island National Park. Green Gables House is located in Cavendish.

"...we have no end of 'times' in fairyland. Spring-
time, long time, short time, new-moon time, good-
night time, next time...but no last time, because that
is too sad a time for fairyland; old time, young time...
because if there is an old time there ought to be a
young time, too; mountain time...because that has
such a fascinating sound; night-time and day-time...
but no bed-time or school-time..."

Anne of Windy Poplars

It was what Susan called a streaky winter...all thaws and freezes that kept Ingleside decorated with fantastic fringes of icicles. The children fed seven bluejays who came regularly to the orchard for their rations and let Jem pick them up, though they flew from everybody else. Anne sat up o' nights to pore over seed catalogues in January and February. Then the winds of March swirled over the dunes and up the harbors and over the hills. Rabbits, said Susan, were laying Easter eggs.

Anne of Ingleside

F<small>Things to do in</small> EBRUARY *19___*

Date	16
1	17
2	18
3	19
4	20
5	21
6	22
7	23
8	24
9	25
10	26
11	27
12	28
13	29
14	
15	

"It must be lovely to be grown up, Marilla, when just being treated as if you were is so nice."

Anne of Green Gables

The two little white-clad figures flew down the long room, through the spare room door, and bounded on the bed at the same moment. And then—something— moved beneath them, there was a gasp and a cry— and somebody said in muffled accents:

"Merciful goodness!"

Anne of Green Gables

_____

_____

_____

_____

_____

_____

_____

_____

_____

_____

_____

_____

_____

_____

_____

_____

_____

_____

_____

_____

_____

_____

_____

_____

''There's really no fun in being sensible *all* the time, Diana.''

Anne of Ingleside

Green Gables House

In the 1930's, the government of Canada developed plans to preserve the area around Cavendish (the community where L. M. Montgomery spent her childhood) by making it part of a national park on the north shore of Prince Edward Island. Although the Green Gables House located here is not exactly the same as the one described in the Anne books, it is very similar to the farmhouse where Anne lived. And when she was a child, Lucy Maud Montgomery, or Maud as she was known to her friends, spent much time at this very house, which was then owned by her cousins. Around the house are many of the spots that Maud, and Anne, loved—Lovers' Lane, the Haunted Wood, Dryad's Bubble and the Birch Path. The inside of the house has been furnished the way it would have looked in Anne's day, and visitors can see the old typewriter that L. M. Montgomery used to type many of her manuscripts. Across the road from Green Gables House is the Cavendish Cemetery, where Maud Montgomery is buried.

At first L. M. Montgomery didn't much like the idea of tourists trampling over "all of those lands and woods-encircled fields where I roved for years." But she eventually realized that the park would prevent the area from being sold to people who might want to develop it or cut down the trees. Today, hundreds of thousands of tourists visit Green Gables House each summer and follow Anne's footsteps through her favorite haunts.

Green Gables House in Cavendish, Prince Edward Island.

"I don't think I've ever been lonely in my life....
Even when I'm alone I have real good company —
dreams and imaginations and pretendings. I *like* to be
alone now and then, just to think over things and
taste them."

Anne's House of Dreams

March came in that winter like the meekest and mildest of lambs, bringing days that were crisp and golden and tingling, each followed by a frosty pink twilight which gradually lost itself in an elfland of moonshine.

Anne of the Island

M *Things to do in* *ARCH* *19*___

Date	16
1	17
2	18
3	19
4	20
5	21
6	22
7	23
8	24
9	25
10	26
11	27
12	28
13	29
14	30
15	31

"Would you like to be a gull? I think I would—that is,
if I couldn't be a human girl. Don't you think it would
be nice to wake up at sunrise and swoop down over
the water and away out over that lovely blue all day;
and then at night to fly back to one's nest?
Oh, I can just imagine myself doing it."

Anne of Green Gables

"Mercy on us," said astonished Marilla, "have you been asleep, Anne?"

"No," was the muffled reply.

"Are you sick then?" demanded Marilla anxiously, going over to the bed.

Anne cowered deeper into her pillows as if desirous of hiding herself for ever from mortal eyes.

"No. But please, Marilla, go away and don't look at me. I'm in the depths of despair and I don't care who gets head in class or writes the best composition or sings in the Sunday school choir any more. Little things like that are of no importance now because I don't suppose I'll ever be able to go anywhere again. My career is closed. Please, Marilla, go away and don't look at me."

"Did any one ever hear the like?" the mystified Marilla wanted to know. "Anne Shirley, whatever is the matter with you? What have you done? Get right up this minute and tell me. This minute, I say. There now what is it?"

Anne slid to the floor in despairing obedience.

"Look at my hair, Marilla," she whispered.

Accordingly, Marilla lifted her candle and looked scrutinizingly at Anne's hair, flowing in heavy masses down her back. It certainly had a very strange appearance.

"Anne Shirley, what have you done to your hair? Why, it's *green*!"

Anne of Green Gables

"This world would be a much more interesting
place...although it *is* very interesting anyhow...
if people spoke out their real thoughts."

Anne of Avonlea

LADY'S SLIPPER
The Floral Emblem of P.E.I.

"Everything is new in the spring," said Anne. "Springs themselves are always so new, too. No spring is ever just like any other spring. It always has something of its own to be its own peculiar sweetness."

Anne of the Island

Anne's Room

When Marilla had gone Anne looked around her wistfully. The whitewashed walls were so painfully bare and staring that she thought they must ache over their own bareness. The floor was bare, too, except for a round braided mat in the middle such as Anne had never seen before. In one corner was the bed, a high, old-fashioned one, with four dark, low-turned posts. In the other corner was the aforesaid three-cornered table adorned with a fat, red velvet pin-cushion hard enough to turn the point of the most adventurous pin. Above it hung a little six by eight mirror. Midway between table and bed was the window, with an icy white muslin frill over it, and opposite it was the washstand. The whole apartment was of a rigidity not to be described in words, but which sent a shiver to the very marrow of Anne's bones. With a sob she hastily discarded her garments, put on the skimpy nightgown and sprang into bed where she burrowed face downward into the pillow and pulled the clothes over her head.

Anne of Green Gables

When Anne first arrived at Green Gables, her room was as bare and unfriendly as her welcome. But gradually Anne and Marilla fixed it up and decorated it, turning it into a place where Anne spent many happy hours—chatting with Diana, getting ready for parties, having friends to sleep over, or just sitting and daydreaming by the window. Today, in Green Gables House on Prince Edward Island, the room that Lucy Maud Montgomery imagined to be Anne's room has been furnished according to the way it looked a few years later:

The floor was covered with a pretty matting, and the curtains that softened the high window and fluttered in the vagrant breezes were of pale green art muslin. The walls, hung not with gold and silver brocade tapestry, but with a dainty apple blossom paper, were adorned with a few good pictures given Anne by Mrs. Allan. Miss Stacy's photograph occupied the place of honor, and Anne made a sentimental point of keeping fresh flowers on the bracket under it. Tonight a spike of white lilies faintly perfumed the room like the dream of a fragrance. There was no "mahogany furniture," but there was a white-painted bookcase filled with books, a cushioned wicker rocker, a toilet table befrilled with white muslin, a quaint, gilt-framed mirror with chubby pink cupids and purple grapes painted over its arched top, that used to hang in the spare room, and a low white bed.

Anne of Green Gables

Anne's Room as recreated in Green Gables House.

"I know I talk too much, but I am really trying to overcome it, and although I say far too much, yet if you only knew how many things I want to say and don't, you'd give me some credit for it."

Anne of Green Gables

April came tiptoeing in beautifully that year with
sunshine and soft winds for a few days; and then a
driving northeast snowstorm dropped a white
blanket over the world again. "Snow in April is
abominable," said Anne. "Like a slap in the face
when you expected a kiss." Ingleside was fringed
with icicles and for two long weeks the days were
raw and the nights hardbitten. Then the snow grudg-
ingly disappeared and when the news went round
that the first robin had been seen in the Hollow
Ingleside plucked up heart and ventured to believe
that the miracle of spring was really going to
happen again.

Anne of Ingleside

A Things to do in
*A*PRIL 19___

Date		16	
1		17	
2		18	
3		19	
4		20	
5		21	
6		22	
7		23	
8		24	
9		25	
10		26	
11		27	
12		28	
13		29	
14		30	
15			

"Isn't it good to be alive on a day like this? I pity the people who aren't born yet for missing it. They may have good days, of course, but they can never have this one."

Anne of Green Gables

For a few minutes Anne, drifting slowly down,
enjoyed the romance of her situation to the full.
Then something happened not at all romantic.
The flat began to leak.

Anne of Green Gables

LILY-OF-THE-VALLEY

"I love to smell flowers in the dark....You get hold of
their soul then."

Anne's House of Dreams

Anne in the Kitchen

While she lived at Green Gables, Anne had some magnificent disasters in the kitchen, including a pudding sauce that contained a drowned mouse, and a cake flavored with liniment, which she served to the minister's wife. But with a great deal of practice and Marilla's help, she eventually became a very good cook.

Like many girls in her day, Anne spent a lot of time in the kitchen, where she learned to clean, cook and make a perfect cup of tea, according to Marilla's high standards. She even enjoyed washing dishes. ("It's fun to make dirty things clean and shining again.") In those days the kitchen was the most important and busiest room in the house—during the cold months there was usually something baking in the oven or sizzling on the wood stove—the heat from the stove helped to warm the house! There were no freezers back then, but in the Green Gables' dark country cellar Anne could search for sweet russet apples to munch, even in the middle of winter. In the summer and fall Marilla would make her famous plum preserves (and her infamous raspberry cordial!) and Anne would make sandwiches and cakes and lemonade to share with her friends on an afternoon picnic.

In *The Anne of Green Gables Cookbook* by Kate Macdonald (Oxford, 1985), there are many recipes inspired by the Anne books, including this delicious recipe for homemade vanilla ice cream, which Anne tasted for the first time at the Sunday school picnic.

"I have never tasted ice cream. Diana tried to explain what it was like, but I guess ice cream is one of those things that are beyond imagination."

Anne of Green Gables

Light and Creamy Vanilla Ice Cream

INGREDIENTS

2 teaspoons gelatin (10 mL)
¼ cup cold water (50 mL)
1 cup milk (250 mL)
½ cup sugar (125 mL)
3 tablespoons corn syrup (45 mL)

1 teaspoon flour (5 mL)
a pinch of salt
1 egg (separated)
2 cups whipping cream (500 mL)
1 tablespoon pure vanilla (15 mL)

YOU WILL NEED

- *double boiler*
- *measuring spoons*
- *measuring cups*
- *small saucepan*

- *wooden spoon*
- *2 small mixing bowls*
- *fork*
- *wire strainer*

- *electric mixer*
- *2 large mixing bowls*
- *rubber spatula*
- *metal bowl* or *pan*

1. Put the whipping cream, electric beaters, and one of the large mixing bowls in the refrigerator to chill.
2. Put about 2 inches (5 cm) of water in the bottom of the double boiler and bring to a boil.
3. Put the gelatin and the cold water in the top pot of the double boiler. Let the gelatin soften for 5 minutes away from the stove.
4. Meanwhile, pour the milk into the small saucepan and place it over medium low heat. When tiny bubbles form around the edge of the pot, the milk is ready.
5. To the gelatin in the top pot of the double boiler add the hot milk, sugar, corn syrup, flour, and salt. Place over the bottom pot containing the boiling water.
6. Stir constantly with the wooden spoon until the mixture thickens— about 15 minutes.
7. Put the lid on and cook the mixture over boiling water for another 10 minutes.
8. Meanwhile, separate the egg into the 2 small mixing bowls. Set aside the egg white for later.
9. Beat the egg yolk **slightly** with a fork. When the 10 minutes are up stir the egg yolk **very slowly** into the mixture on top of the stove. Cook and stir for 1 more minute.
10. Pour the hot ice cream mixture through a wire strainer into the other large mixing bowl.
11. When the ice cream mixture has cooled to room temperature, beat it with the electric mixer until it is light and creamy—about 5 minutes.
12. In the chilled large mixing bowl whip the cold whipping cream with the electric mixer until it falls in large globs and forms a soft peak.
13. Rinse the beaters thoroughly with hot water. Then beat the egg white until it is stiff and glossy but not dry.
14. Very gently with the rubber spatula, fold first the whipped cream, then the egg white into the ice cream mixture. Gently stir in the vanilla.
15. Spoon the mixture into the metal bowl or pan and place in the freezer. Freeze for about 3 or 4 hours—until firm.

ASSORTED WILDFLOWERS

"What is an imagination for if not to enable you to peep at life through other people's eyes?"

Anne of Avonlea

Spring had come once more to Green Gables—the beautiful, capricious, reluctant Canadian spring, lingering along through April and May in a succession of sweet, fresh, chilly days, with pink sunsets and miracles of resurrection and growth. The maples in Lovers' Lane were red-budded and little curly ferns pushed up around the Dryad's Bubble. Away up in the barrens, behind Mr. Silas Sloane's place, the Mayflowers blossomed out, pink and white stars of sweetness under their brown leaves. All the school girls and boys had one golden afternoon gathering them, coming home in the clear, echoing twilight with arms and baskets full of flowery spoil.

Anne of Green Gables

*M*AY 19___

Things to do in

Date	16
1	17
2	18
3	19
4	20
5	21
6	22
7	23
8	24
9	25
10	26
11	27
12	28
13	29
14	30
15	31

"There's just one spot on this road where I always
feel suddenly...'I'm *home*,'" said Anne. "It's the top
of the next hill, where we'll see the lights of Green
Gables. I'm just thinking of the supper Marilla will
have ready for us. I believe I can smell it here. Oh, it's
good...good...good to be home again!"

At Green Gables every tree in the yard seemed
to welcome her back...every lighted window was
beckoning. And how good Marilla's kitchen smelled
as they opened the door. There were hugs and
exclamations and laughter.

Anne of Windy Poplars

CANADIAN PRIMROSE

"It's really splendid to imagine you are a queen.
You have all the fun of it without any of the incon-
veniences and you can stop being a queen whenever
you want to, which you couldn't in real life."

Anne of Avonlea

"Will you swear to be my friend for ever and ever?"
demanded Anne eagerly.

Anne of Green Gables

TIGER LILIES

"Marilla, isn't it nice to think that tomorrow is a new day with no mistakes in it yet?"

"I'll warrant you'll make plenty in it," said Marilla. "I never saw your beat for making mistakes, Anne."

"Yes, and well I know it," admitted Anne mournfully. "But have you ever noticed one encouraging thing about me, Marilla? I never make the same mistake twice."

"I don't know as that's much benefit when you're always making new ones."

"Oh, don't you see, Marilla? There *must* be a limit to the mistakes one person can make, and when I get to the end of them, then I'll be through with them. That's a very comforting thought."

Anne of Green Gables

APPLE BLOSSOMS

"I'm sure no life can be properly developed and
rounded out without some trial and sorrow – though
I suppose it is only when we are pretty comfortable
that we admit it."

Anne of the Island

"I wonder what it would be like to live in a world where it was always June..."

Anne of the Island

Things to do in
JUNE *19*___

Date	16
1	17
2	18
3	19
4	20
5	21
6	22
7	23
8	24
9	25
10	26
11	27
12	28
13	29
14	30
15	

_____

_____

_____

_____

_____

_____

_____

_____

_____

_____

_____

_____

_____

_____

_____

_____

_____

_____

_____

_____

_____

"Kindred spirits are not so scarce as I used to think. It's splendid to find out there are so many of them in the world."

Anne of Green Gables

A child of about eleven, garbed in a very short,
very tight, very ugly dress of yellowish gray wincey.
She wore a faded brown sailor hat and beneath the
hat, extending down her back, were two braids of
very thick, decidedly red hair. Her face was small,
white and thin, also much freckled; her mouth was
large and so were her eyes, that looked green in some
lights and moods and gray in others.

Anne of Green Gables

ROSES

"Do you know when and where I'd like to be
married, if I could? It would be at dawn — a June
dawn, with a glorious sunrise, and roses blooming in
the gardens..."

Anne's House of Dreams

Anne's Flowers

"The year is a book, isn't it, Marilla? Spring's pages
are written in Mayflowers and violets, summer's in
roses, autumn's in red maple leaves, and winter in
holly and evergreen."

Anne of the Island

Anne loved flowers. She was always gathering them
to decorate her room, wearing them in her hair or
pinned to her coat or dress, bringing bouquets to
friends, or simply admiring the flowers that grew
wild everywhere on Prince Edward Island—from the
June lilies and bleeding hearts at Windy Poplars to the
wild strawberries of Mr. Harrison's pasture and the
ferns in the Haunted Wood. These are just some of the
flowers that were special to Anne:

apple blossoms: Even though they
never lasted long once they were
brought indoors, Anne would often
collect fragrant apple blossoms and
put them in a vase. She even had an
apple blossom pattern on the wall-
paper of her room.

daffodils: Anne's walk at Ingleside
was lined with daffodils every spring.
Sometimes called narcissi, these
trumpet-shaped flowers also grew in
one of Anne's favorite spots in Avonlea
—Hester Gray's abandoned garden,
which every spring would be a "sheet
of yellow and white narcissi, in their
airiest, most lavish, wind-swayed
bloom." Daffodils are also called Lent
lilies, because in their native England
they bloomed shortly before Easter
and were used to decorate churches.
During Shakespeare's time, in the
spring, daffodils were sold for a penny
a bunch by London flower women
who carried the flowers in large
wicker baskets balanced on their heads.

daisies: During the summer, the field
between Anne's house and Leslie
Moore's place was "white as snow
with daisies." These yellow-centered
white flowers are also called moon
pennies, marguerites or ox-eye daisies.
In the Middle Ages, the flowers and
leaves were used to make tea.

heather: While strolling through the
Kingsport park with her friends, Anne
was delighted to learn that the park
contained a rare patch of heather.
Heather is native to the British Isles,
where it grows on moors and heaths
(hence its name), producing tiny purple bell-shaped flowers in the autumn.

lavender: Anne's good friend,
Miss Lavendar, lived at Echo Lodge,
a house surrounded by the sweet-
scented plant she was named after.
Lavender is a kind of fragrant mint.
It has purple flowers that are often
dried and used in sachets or perfumes.
In Victorian times, young women
would scent their foreheads and hand-

kerchiefs with lavender, in the belief that it would keep them chaste.

lilies: Anne would often keep fresh lilies beneath the photo of Miss Stacy, her teacher. The name comes from the Celtic word, *li,* meaning whiteness. It was a sacred flower in ancient Crete and from early times has stood for motherhood, fruitfulness and light. In North America there are over two thousand species of lilies.

lilies-of-the-valley: Anne wore lilies-of-the-valley in her hair at Diana's wedding and carried a bouquet of them that Gilbert had sent her to her college graduation. These delicate and very fragrant flowers bloom in early spring. In ancient Greece and Rome, women would use distilled water made from lilies-of-the-valley as a skin tonic.

pansies: When Anne walked through the old graveyard located across the street from her boarding house in Kingsport, she unpinned a cluster of purple pansies that she wore and placed them on the grave of a boy who had died in a war at sea. The name pansy comes from the French *pensées*, meaning thoughts. It is also called heartsease and love-in-idleness.

peonies: In June, Anne would cut vasefuls of peonies. She especially liked the milky-white ones with the "blood-red flecks at their hearts, like a god's kiss." Named after Paeon, a favorite physician of the Greek gods, it was once used as a medicinal plant, and in cooking. Peony seeds were also once considered a charm against evil.

roses: Anne carried roses on her wedding day. As Owen Ford said when he proposed to Leslie Moore, "The rose is the flower of love—the world has acclaimed it so for centuries. The pink rose is love hopeful and expectant—the white roses are love dead or forsaken—but the red roses...are...love triumphant and perfect."

violets: Anne loved violets, especially those that grew in her beloved Violet Vale, which looked like a "big bowlful of violets" every May. Anne's favorite pupil, Paul Irving, thought that violets were "little snips of the sky that fell down when the angels cut out holes for the stars to shine through," and Anne's friend Priscilla once said that if a kiss could be seen, it would look like a violet. There are so many species of violets that some member of the violet family grows in every part of the world, even in the Arctic and Antarctic. The violet was the symbol of ancient Greece—the Greeks used it for decorations and perfumes. Violets are even edible, and are sometimes used in candies or salads. Though they have a sweet fragrance, there is a substance in the flower that lessens the sense of smell after a short time, so that it seems as if the flower's scent fades quickly. If you inhale the flower after a few moments, it will smell fragrant again.

WILD STRAWBERRIES

"School closed today. Two months of Green Gables
and dew-wet, spicy ferns ankle-deep along the brook
and lazy, dappling shadows in Lover's Lane and wild
strawberries in Mr. Bell's pasture and the dark love-
liness of firs in the Haunted Wood! My very soul
has wings."

Anne of Windy Poplars

All in all, it was a never-to-be-forgotten summer—
one of those summers which come seldom into any
life, but leave a rich heritage of beautiful memories in
their going—one of those summers which, in a fortu-
nate combination of delightful weather, delightful
friends and delightful doings, come as near to
perfection as anything can come in this world.

Anne's House of Dreams

J *Things to do in* *ULY 19*

Date		16	
1		17	
2		18	
3		19	
4		20	
5		21	
6		22	
7		23	
8		24	
9		25	
10		26	
11		27	
12		28	
13		29	
14		30	
15		31	

FIELD CHICKWEED

"...tears can be happy as well as sad. My very
happiest moments have been when I had tears in my
eyes..."

Anne's House of Dreams

Anne climbed the ladder amid breathless silence, gained the ridge pole, balanced herself uprightly on that precarious footing, and started to walk along it, dizzily conscious that she was uncomfortably high up in the world and that walking ridgepoles was not a thing in which your imagination helped you out much. Nevertheless, she managed to take several steps before the catastrophe came. Then she swayed, lost her balance, stumbled, staggered and fell, sliding down over the sun-baked roof and crashing off it through the tangle of Virginia creeper beneath — all before the dismayed circle below could give a simultaneous, terrified shriek.

Anne of Green Gables

"There's such a lot of different Annes in me. I sometimes think that is why I'm such a troublesome person. If I was just the one Anne it would be ever so much more comfortable, but then it wouldn't be half so interesting."

Anne of Green Gables

Anne's Dictionary

One of the reasons the Anne books are still so popular today is that Anne is in many ways a modern girl — her dreams, disappointments and ambitions are timeless. But she did live almost one hundred years ago, when the people of Prince Edward Island lived without modern-day comforts such as electric stoves, automobiles and central heating. In the Anne books you'll find several terms and expressions that are not very common today.

anodyne liniment: When Anne made a cake for Mrs. Allan, she mistakenly put anodyne liniment in it instead of vanilla. Anodyne liniment was an oily liquid that was rubbed on the skin to ease muscle pain.

calico: During freshman initiation at college, Gilbert Blythe had to parade down the streets of Kingsport wearing a bonnet and flowered calico apron made of cotton material with a many-colored pattern on it.

catechism: In Anne's day, children who went to Sunday school had to learn catechism. They would learn by heart answers to questions about religion and then had to recite the answers from memory.

chloroform: This thin, colorless liquid was often used as an anesthetic — when the fumes were inhaled, a person would become unconscious. Anne and her college friends tried to chloroform Rusty, the stray cat that followed Anne home one day. A knothole in the box saved his life, and he eventually became a favorite pet.

consumption: Ruby Gillis died of what Mrs. Lynde called "galloping consumption," which is what people called tuberculosis — a serious lung disease that in those days was usually fatal.

cordial: When Anne invited Diana to tea, she *planned* to serve her raspberry cordial, a thick, tangy raspberry fruit juice.

cowcumbers: When Miss Sarah Copp invited Anne and Diana to tea, she warned them to expect nothing more than bread, butter and cowcumbers — cucumbers!

coxcomb: In Anne's day, coxcomb was the term used to describe a conceited and foolish person, usually a man.

crimpers: Gilbert's cranky old Aunt Mary Maria wore her crimpers to bed every night — old-fashioned hair curlers. Susan claimed that the shadow of her head looked as if it had horns, like the devil himself!

dinky: When Ruby Gillis told Anne once that her hat was "real dinky," she meant it was neat, pretty and dainty.

hogshead: Aunt Mary Maria Blythe was so mean that Anne's children named a doll with a split head after her. Whenever Aunt Mary Maria scolded them, they would go out and drown the doll in the hogshead — a huge barrel kept for collecting rainwater.

ipecac: When Minnie May Barry had croup, Anne saved her life by treating her with ipecac — a medicine that makes one vomit.

jackstones: In Anne's day, children would use small smooth stones — jackstones — for playing the game of jacks.

jamboree: When Anne went to visit her friend Philippa, she became caught up in Phil's busy social life of "jamborees"—picnics, parties, dances and celebrations of various kinds.

kittle-cattle: After Anne was sent ten dollars by a magazine that published a piece she wrote, her friend Priscilla teased her by claiming that all authors were kittle-cattle, or difficult to deal with, and now Anne would probably become the same way.

latch-string: Anne used to say that her latch-string was "always out" for kindred spirits. In those days a catch or latch held doors and gates closed. A string attached to the latch could be left hanging outside the door to allow visitors to lift the latch and enter, or be drawn inside the door to prevent people from coming in.

ploughshare: When Owen Ford told Anne that he was in love with Leslie Moore, he said that it would be easier to walk over "red hot ploughshares" than leave Leslie. A ploughshare is the sharp, pointed metal part of a plough, which digs into the soil.

poll-parrot: In Anne's day, a poll-parrot was someone who kept repeating things, just like a tame parrot.

potatoes and point: When Captain Jim gave his steak dinner to a stray dog, he was left with nothing but "potatoes and point" for himself—an expression for a meager meal, because one could only point to the spot on the plate where the meat was supposed to be!

pung sleigh: For Diana's birthday, Anne was allowed to go to the Debating Club concert, travelling in a pung sleigh—a big sleigh with a box-shaped body. The word *pung* comes from the North American Indian word, *tom-pung,* similar to the word *toboggan,* which is also of Indian origin.

ridge pole: When Anne accepted the dare to walk the Barry's ridge pole, she walked along the very top, pointed part of the roof. When she fell off, she slid down the roof and tumbled off it into the bushes below.

saddle-board: The day Davy skipped Sunday school, he spent the morning being naughty at the Cotton family's house, where he cut his initials on the saddle-board of the pig-house. The saddle-board was the strip of metal that covered the pointed part of the roof.

swain: In Anne's day, boyfriends or admirers were called swains. A "smitten swain" was a boy who was particularly in love.

tallow: At Four Winds, Miss Cornelia would advise rubbing tallow, or animal fat, on one's nose as treatment for a cold. Tallow was also used for making soap and candles.

tick: On the day that a well-known writer unexpectedly came to visit, Anne was in the middle of transferring feathers from her old bed tick, or mattress, to a new one. All the feathers had to be removed from the old mattress covering and shifted to a new case. It was a messy job at best, and Anne was covered with feathers and down when her famous guest arrived!

twit: After Anne's famous first meeting with Mrs. Rachel Lynde, Marilla told Rachel she shouldn't have "twitted" Anne about her looks—teased or criticized her.

wincey: When Anne first arrived in Avonlea, she was wearing a "very short, very tight, very ugly dress of yellowish gray wincey"—a thick, plain fabric made of wool and cotton, which was often used for making pajamas.

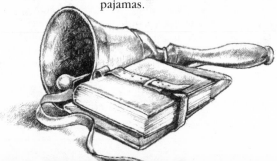

"I think an old, deserted house is such a sad sight," said Anne dreamily. "It always seems to me to be thinking about its past and mourning for its old-time joys."

Anne of Avonlea

The garret was a shadowy, suggestive, delightful place, as all garrets should be. Through the open window, by which Anne sat, blew the sweet, scented, sun-warm air of the August afternoon; outside, poplar boughs rustled and tossed in the wind; beyond them were the woods, where Lover's Lane wound its enchanted path, and the old apple orchard which still bore its rosy harvests munificently. And, over all, was a great mountain range of snowy clouds in the blue southern sky. Through the other window was glimpsed a distant, white-capped, blue sea—the beautiful St. Lawrence Gulf, on which floats, like a jewel, Abegweit, whose softer, sweeter Indian name has long been forsaken for the more prosaic one of Prince Edward Island.

Anne's House of Dreams

A Things to do in AUGUST 19___

Date	16
1	17
2	18
3	19
4	20
5	21
6	22
7	23
8	24
9	25
10	26
11	27
12	28
13	29
14	30
15	31

WATER LILY

"It's a pretty good world, after all, isn't it, Marilla?
concluded Anne happily. "Mrs. Lynde was complain-
ing the other day that it wasn't much of a world. She
said whenever you looked forward to anything pleas-
ant you were sure to be more or less disappointed
...that nothing ever came up to your expectations.
Well, perhaps that is true. But there is a good side to it
too. The bad things don't always come up to your
expectations either...they nearly always turn out ever
so much better than you think."

Anne of Avonlea

"Have you any unfulfilled dreams, Anne?" asked Gilbert.

Something in his tone...made Anne's heart beat wildly.

Anne of the Island

"Isn't it splendid to think of all the things there are to find out about? It just makes me feel glad to be alive—it's such an interesting world. It wouldn't be half so interesting if we knew all about everything, would it? There'd be no scope for imagination then, would there?"

Anne of Green Gables

FIREWEED

_____

_____

_____

_____

_____

_____

_____

_____

_____

_____

_____

_____

_____

_____

_____

_____

_____

_____

_____

_____

_____

_____

"And yet...it's the little things that fret the holes in life...like moths...and ruin it."

Anne of Ingleside

Portraits of Anne

Public opinion never agreed on Anne's looks.
People who had heard her called handsome met her
and were disappointed. People who had heard her
called plain saw her and wondered where other
people's eyes were.

Anne of Avonlea

Anne has been depicted by many artists since *Anne of
Green Gables* was first published in 1908. In addition
to her famous red hair, she had freckles, a pale com-
plexion, broad forehead, handsome nose, and eyes
"that looked green in some lights and moods and gray
in others." Anne's hairstyle and clothes changed
through the years (she wore her hair in braids or loose
as a young girl, and when she got older she wore it
pinned up). Though she wasn't a classic beauty like
her friend Diana, there was something stylish and
spirited about her that made her stand out in a
crowd—"She seemed to walk in an atmosphere of
things about to happen."

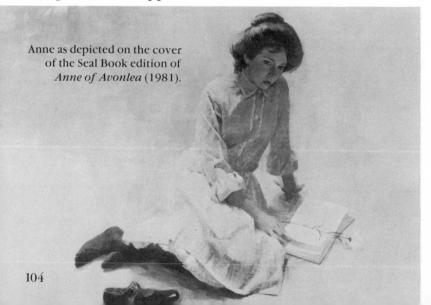

Anne as depicted on the cover
of the Seal Book edition of
Anne of Avonlea (1981).

Anne as depicted by George Gibbs in *Anne of Avonlea* (1909).

Here is Anne as M.L. Kirk imagines her in *Anne's House of Dreams* (1917).

This Canadian stamp was issued on May 15, 1975.

BLACK-EYED SUSANS

"You set your heart too much on things, Anne," said Marilla with a sigh. "I'm afraid there'll be a great many disappointments in store for you through life."

"Oh, Marilla, looking forward to things is half the pleasure of them," exclaimed Anne. "You mayn't get the things themselves; but nothing can prevent you from having the fun of looking forward to them."

Anne of Green Gables

A September day on Prince Edward Island hills; a crisp wind blowing up over the sand dunes from the sea; a long red road, winding through fields and woods, now looping itself about a corner of thick set spruces, now threading a plantation of young maples with great feathery sheets of ferns beneath them, now dipping down into a hollow where a brook flashed out of the woods and into them again, now basking in open sunshine between ribbons of golden-rod and smoke-blue asters; air athrill with the pipings of myriads of crickets, those glad little pensioners of the summer hills; a plump brown pony ambling along the road; two girls behind him, full to the lips with the simple, priceless joy of youth and life."

Anne of Avonlea

*S*Things to do in
*S*EPTEMBER 19___

Date	16
1	17
2	18
3	19
4	20
5	21
6	22
7	23
8	24
9	25
10	26
11	27
12	28
13	29
14	30
15	

"But we can't have things perfect in this
imperfect world, as Mrs. Lynde says. Mrs. Lynde
isn't exactly a comforting person sometimes,
but there's no doubt she says a great many
very true things."

Anne of Green Gables

Gilbert reached across the aisle, picked up the end of Anne's long red braid, held it out at arm's length and said in a piercing whisper,

"Carrots! Carrots!"

Then Anne looked at him with a vengeance!

She did more than look. She sprang to her feet, her bright fancies fallen into cureless ruin. She flashed one indignant glance at Gilbert from eyes whose angry sparkle was swiftly quenched in equally angry tears.

"You mean, hateful boy!" she exclaimed passionately. "How dare you!"

And then — Thwack! Anne had brought her slate down on Gilbert's head and cracked it — slate, not head — clear across.

Anne of Green Gables

_____

_____

_____

_____

_____

_____

_____

_____

_____

_____

_____

_____

_____

_____

_____

_____

_____

_____

_____

_____

_____

_____

_____

_____

_____

"There's all the difference in the world, you know, between being inside looking out and outside looking in."

Anne of Windy Poplars

115

Writing *Anne of Green Gables*

L. M. Montgomery started writing *Anne of Green
Gables* in the spring of 1904. She had never written a
whole book before, but she had written hundreds of
poems, short stories, newspaper articles and columns.
"I have always hated beginning a story," she wrote.
"When I get the first paragraph written I feel as
though it were half done. The rest comes easily. To
begin a book, therefore, seemed quite a stupendous
task." Maud kept a notebook filled with ideas for
plots, characters and descriptions, and one day she
found a note in her journal about an orphan girl who
is mistakenly sent to an elderly couple instead of a boy.
This idea eventually grew into *Anne of Green Gables.*

 L. M. Montgomery wrote the book in the evenings
after she got home from her newspaper job, and fin-
ished it a year and a half later. The manuscript was
rejected by five publishers. Discouraged, Maud put
the novel away for several months, and then decided
to try one more publisher. This one accepted it. Little
did she know then that she would end up writing five
more books about Anne, and that *Anne of Green
Gables* would eventually be read by millions of readers in sixty countries around the world, and would be
translated into thirty-six languages.

This is the first page of the first chapter of *Anne of Green Gables* that Lucy Maud Montgomery began writing by hand in 1904.

_____

_____

_____

_____

_____

_____

_____

_____

_____

_____

_____

_____

_____

_____

_____

_____

_____

_____

_____

_____

One day a wind blew through the Ingleside garden...
the first wind of autumn. That night the rose of the
sunset was a trifle austere. All at once the summer
had grown old. The turn of the season had come.

Anne of Ingleside

It was...a glorious October, all red and gold, with mellow mornings when the valleys were filled with delicate mists as if the spirit of autumn had poured them in for the sun to drain—amethyst, pearl, silver, rose, and smoke-blue. The dews were so heavy that the fields glistened like cloth of silver and there were such heaps of rustling leaves in the hollows of many-stemmed woods to run crisply through. The Birch Path was a canopy of yellow and the ferns were sear and brown all along it. There was a tang in the very air that inspired the hearts of small maidens tripping, unlike snails, swiftly and willingly to school; and it *was* jolly to be back again at the little brown desk beside Diana, with Ruby Gillis nodding across the aisle and Carrie Sloane sending up notes and Julia Bell passing a "chew" of gum down from the back seat. Anne drew a long breath of happiness as she sharpened her pencil and arranged her picture cards in her desk. Life was certainly very interesting.

Anne of Green Gables

Things to do in
OCTOBER 19__

Date		16	
1		17	
2		18	
3		19	
4		20	
5		21	
6		22	
7		23	
8		24	
9		25	
10		26	
11		27	
12		28	
13		29	
14		30	
15		31	

SUNFLOWER

Say what you will, thought Anne, there is always
something a little strange about a moonlit room.
Its whole personality is changed. It is not so
friendly...so human. It is remote and aloof and
wrapped up in itself. Almost it regards you as
an intruder.

Anne of Ingleside

She caught up her skirt and pirouetted along the hard strip of sand just out of reach of the waves that almost lapped her feet with their spent foam. Whirling round and round, laughing like a child, she reached the little headland that ran out to the east of the cove; then she stopped suddenly, blushing crimson; she was not alone; there had been a witness to her dance and laughter.

The girl of the golden hair and sea-blue eyes was sitting on a boulder of the headland, half-hidden by a jutting rock. She was looking straight at Anne with a strange expression—part wonder, part sympathy, part—could it be?—envy.

Anne's House of Dreams

Anne was always glad in the happiness of her friends;
but it is sometimes a little lonely to be surrounded
everywhere by a happiness that is not your own.

Anne of the Island

_____

_____

_____

_____

_____

_____

_____

_____

_____

_____

_____

_____

_____

_____

_____

_____

_____

_____

_____

_____

_____

_____

_____

_____

''I think the little things in life often make more
trouble than the big things...''

Anne of Avonlea

L. M. Montgomery

Lucy Maud Montgomery was born at Clifton, Prince Edward Island, in 1874. When Maud was very small, her mother died of tuberculosis. Maud was raised by her grandparents after her widowed father moved to Saskatchewan.

Like Anne, Maud went to teacher's college in Prince Edward Island and university in Nova Scotia. Later she taught school and worked for a newspaper in Halifax. She wrote many short pieces but did not become well known until *Anne of Green Gables* was published in 1908. In 1911 she married a minister, Rev. Ewan Macdonald, and continued to write while raising two sons. She spent the last half of her life in Ontario, and died in 1942.

Although the Anne books are not based heavily on L. M. Montgomery's own life, there are many similarities. Like Anne, Maud believed in fairies, loved naming flowers, trees and her favorite spots, had an imaginary friend who lived in a bookcase, and hated to be teased or humiliated. She attended a one-room school in Cavendish, where she would put her bottle of milk in the brook every day to keep cool.

L. M. Montgomery wanted to be a writer from the time she was very young, and she was always writing stories and poems. She also formed a story club with her friends. Many of her poems were about the outdoors—the seasons, stars, trees and sunsets. These verses are part of a poem she wrote when she was nine years old:

> Around the poplar and the spruce
> The fir and maple stood;
> But the old tree that I loved the best
> Grew in the Haunted Wood.

It was a stately, tall old birch,
With spreading branches green;
It kept off heat and sun and glare—
'Twas a goodly tree, I ween.

'Twas the Monarch of the Forest,
A splendid Kingly Name,
Oh, it was a beautiful birch tree,
A tree that was known to fame.

Although she eventually became a world-famous writer, L. M. Montgomery's career was not an instant success. She was twenty-four before she was making even a small "livable" income from her writing, and throughout her life she said that nine out of the ten things she sent out to publishers still came back. But she never gave up—she would keep submitting her manuscripts until they were accepted.

Maud at age sixteen.

At eleven, Maud was already writing stories and poems.

At nineteen, Maud was studying at teacher's college in Prince Edward Island.

"Oh, it's delightful to have ambitions. I'm so glad
I have such a lot. And there never seems to be any
end to them—that's the best of it. Just as soon as you
attain to one ambition you see another one glittering
higher up still. It does make life so interesting."

Anne of Green Gables

...November closed in on Ingleside. The dark hills, with the darker spruces marching over them, looked grim on early falling nights, but Ingleside bloomed with firelight and laughter, though the winds come in from the Atlantic singing of mournful things....

But some days even the wind blew cheerfully through the silvery grey maple wood and some days there was no wind at all, only mellow Indian summer sunshine and the quiet shadows of the bare trees all over the lawn and frosty stillness at sunset.

Anne of Ingleside

Things to do in NOVEMBER 19___

Date	16
1	17
2	18
3	19
4	20
5	21
6	22
7	23
8	24
9	25
10	26
11	27
12	28
13	29
14	30
15	

DAISIES

"It's really wonderful, Marilla, what you can do when you're truly anxious to please a certain person."

Anne of Green Gables

"In November I sometimes feel as if spring could never come again..."

Anne's House of Dreams

Suddenly the rain of Aunt Jamesina's prophecy came with a swish and rush. Anne put up her umbrella and hurried down the slope. As she turned out on the harbor road a savage gust of wind tore along it. Instantly her umbrella turned wrong side out. Anne clutched at it in despair. And then—there came a voice close to her:

"Pardon me—may I offer you the shelter of my umbrella?"

Anne of the Island

"I don't like places or people either that haven't any faults. I think a truly perfect person would be very uninteresting."

Anne of Avonlea

"November is usually such a disagreeable month...
as if the year had suddenly found out that she was
growing old and could do nothing but weep and fret
over it. This year is growing old gracefully...just like a
stately old lady who knows she can be charming even
with gray hair and wrinkles."

Anne of Avonlea

But on this particular day it seemed as if December
had remembered that it was time for winter and had
turned suddenly dull and brooding, with a windless
hush predictive of coming snow. Nevertheless, Anne
keenly enjoyed her walk through the great gray maze
of the beechlands; though alone she never found it
lonely; her imagination peopled her path with merry
companions, and with these she carried on a gay,
pretended conversation that was wittier and more
fascinating than conversations are apt to be in real
life, where people sometimes fail most lamentably to
talk up to the requirements. In a ''make believe''
assembly of choice spirits everybody says just the
thing you want her to say and so gives you the chance
to say just what *you* want to say. Attended by this
invisible company, Anne traversed the woods and
arrived at the fir lane just as broad, feathery flakes
began to flutter down softly.

Anne of Avonlea

Things to do in
DECEMBER 19___

Date	16
1	17
2	18
3	19
4	20
5	21
6	22
7	23
8	24
9	25
10	26
11	27
12	28
13	29
14	30
15	31

_____

_____

_____

_____

_____

_____

_____

_____

_____

_____

_____

_____

Christmas morning broke on a beautiful white world. It had been a very mild December and people had looked forward to a green Christmas; but just enough snow fell softly in the night to transfigure Avonlea. Anne peeped out from her frosted gable window with delighted eyes. The firs in the Haunted Wood were all feathery and wonderful; the birches and wild cherry trees were outlined in pearl; the ploughed fields were stretches of snowy dimples; and there was a crisp tang in the air that was glorious. Anne ran downstairs singing until her voice reechoed through Green Gables.

"Merry Christmas, Marilla! Merry Christmas, Matthew! Isn't it a lovely Christmas? I'm so glad it's white. Any other kind of Christmas doesn't seem real, does it? I don't like green Christmases. They're *not* green—they're just nasty faded browns and grays."

Anne of Green Gables

POINSETTIA

"I suppose we'll get used to being grown-up in time," said Anne cheerfully. "There won't be so many unexpected things about it by and by—though, after all, I fancy it's the unexpected things that give spice to life."

Anne of the Island

When Anne returned to the school after dinner all the children were as usual in their seats and every face was bent studiously over a desk except Anthony Pye's. He peered across his book at Anne, his black eyes sparkling with curiosity and mockery. Anne twitched open the drawer of her desk in search of chalk and under her very hand a lively mouse sprang out of the drawer, scampered over the desk, and leaped to the floor.

Anne screamed and sprang back, as if it had been a snake, and Anthony Pye laughed aloud.

Then a silence fell... a very creepy, uncomfortable silence. Annetta Bell was of two minds whether to go into hysterics again or not, especially as she didn't know just where the mouse had gone. But she decided not to. Who could take any comfort out of hysterics with a teacher so white-faced and so blazing-eyed standing before one?

"Who put that mouse in my desk?" said Anne. Her voice was quite low but it made a shiver go up and down Paul Irving's spine.

Anne of Avonlea

_____

_____

_____

_____

_____

_____

_____

_____

_____

_____

_____

_____

_____

_____

_____

_____

_____

_____

_____

_____

_____

_____

_____

"Having adventures comes natural to some people,"
said Anne serenely. "You just have a gift for them or
you haven't."

Anne of Avonlea

Books by L. M. Montgomery

After *Anne of Green Gables* was published, readers
wanted to know more about Anne. Eventually
five more books appeared, describing Anne's days
teaching in Avonlea (*Anne of Avonlea*), going to
college (*Anne of the Island*), working as a high-school
principal (*Anne of Windy Poplars*) and her marriage
and children (*Anne's House of Dreams* and *Anne of
Ingleside*). Two additional books—*Rainbow Valley*
(about Anne's children) and *Rilla of Ingleside* (about
Anne's youngest daughter)—were written before
Anne of Windy Poplars and *Anne of Ingleside*.

    L. M. Montgomery also wrote three books about
a solitary aspiring young writer named Emily, and
these books are even more autobiographical than the
Anne books. In all, she wrote over twenty-five books,
including an autobiography and a book of poetry. She
also wrote many short pieces and newspaper articles.

1908	Anne of Green Gables
1909	Anne of Avonlea
1910	Kilmeny of the Orchard
1911	The Story Girl
1912	Chronicles of Avonlea
1913	The Golden Road
1915	Anne of the Island
1916	Anne's House of Dreams
1916	The Watchman and Other Poems
1919	Rainbow Valley
1920	Further Chronicles of Avonlea
1921	Rilla of Ingleside
1923	Emily of New Moon
1924	Emily Climbs
1926	The Blue Castle
1927	Emily's Quest
1929	Magic for Marigold
1931	A Tangled Web

1933	Pat of Silver Bush
1935	Mistress Pat
1936	Anne of Windy Poplars
1937	Jane of Lantern Hill
1939	Anne of Ingleside
1974	The Road to Yesterday
1979	The Doctor's Sweetheart and Other Stories

Books about L. M. Montgomery
The Alpine Path: The Story of My Career—L. M. Montgomery *(1974)*
The Green Gables Letters—Wilfrid Eggleston *(1960)*
Lucy Maud Montgomery: The Island's Lady of Stories
   —The Women's Institute, Springfield, P.E.I. *(1963)*
The Years before "Anne"—Francis W. P. Bolger *(1974)*
The Wheel of Things—Mollie Gillen *(1975)*
The Canadians (L. M. Montgomery)—Mollie Gillen *(1978)*
My Dear Mr. M.: Letters to G. B. MacMillan
   (from L. M. Montgomery 1903-1941)—Francis W. P. Bolger
   and Elizabeth Epperly *(1980)*
The Selected Journals of L.M. Montgomery, Volume I: 1889-1910 —
   Mary Rubio and Elizabeth Waterston *(1985)*

Other Books
Spirit of Place—Francis W. P. Bolger, Wayne Barrett,
   Anne MacKay *(1982)*
A Child's Anne—Deirdre Kestler, Floyd Trainor *(1983)*
Green Gables—Parks and People *(1982)*
The Anne of Green Gables Cookbook—Kate Macdonald *(1985)*

The old year did not slip away in a green twilight,
with a pinky-yellow sunset. Instead, it went out with
a wild, white bluster and blow. It was one of the
nights when the storm-wind hurtles over the frozen
meadows and black hollows, and moans around the
eaves like a lost creature, and drives the snow sharply
against the shaking panes.

"Just the sort of night people like to cuddle down
between their blankets and count their mercies,"
said Anne.

Anne of the Island

Acknowledgements

The publisher would like to thank the following for permission to reproduce material:

Page 29: Prince Edward Island National Park, photographer Barb MacDonald for Green Gables House; page 43: Prince Edward Island National Park, photographer Barb MacDonald for Anne's Room; page 55: "Light and Creamy Vanilla Ice Cream" from *The Anne of Green Gables Cookbook* © Kate Macdonald 1985; reproduced by permission of Oxford University Press Canada; page 104: Bantam Seal Books for the cover illustration from the Seal Book edition of *Anne of Avonlea;* page 105: The Osborne Collection of Early Children's Books, Toronto Public Library for the reproduction of the frontispieces by George Gibbs and M.L. Kirk; page 105: Frontispiece by M.L. Kirk from *Anne's House of Dreams* used by permission of The Canadian Publishers, McClelland and Stewart Limited, Toronto; page 105: 1975 stamp reproduced courtesy of Canada Post Corporation; page 117: First page from manuscript of *Anne of Green Gables* courtesy of the Permanent Collection of the Confederation Centre Art Gallery and Museum in P.E.I.; page 131: Public Archives Canada for the three photographs of L.M. Montgomery at ages 11 (C-66943), 16 (C-66951) and 19 (C-66946). Selections from the works of L.M. Montgomery are used with the permission of Ruth Macdonald; David Macdonald; Farrar, Straus and Giroux Inc.; Harper & Row, Publishers Inc.; and Jack McClelland.

Available from Seal Books:

Anne of Green Gables
Anne of Avonlea
Anne's House of Dreams
Anne of Ingleside
Anne of the Island
Anne of Windy Poplars
Chronicles of Avonlea
Further Chronicles of Avonlea
Emily Climbs
Emily of New Moon
Emily's Quest
The Golden Road

Kilmeny of the Orchard
The Story Girl
Rainbow Valley
Rilla of Ingleside
Jane of Lantern Hill
The Blue Castle
Magic for Marigold
Pat of Silver Bush
Mistress Pat
A Tangled Web
The Anne of Green Gables Cookbook